BISMARK AND US

A True Story

Min Pin Tootsie

authorHOUSE

AuthorHouse™ UK
1663 Liberty Drive
Bloomington, IN 47403 USA
www.authorhouse.co.uk
Phone: 0800.197.4150

© 2016 Min Pin Tootsie. All rights reserved.

No part of this book may be reproduced, stored in a retrieval system, or transmitted by any means without the written permission of the author.

Published by AuthorHouse 04/26/2016

ISBN: 978-1-5246-3266-3 (sc)
ISBN: 978-1-5246-3265-6 (hc)
ISBN: 978-1-5246-3267-0 (e)

Print information available on the last page.

Any people depicted in stock imagery provided by Thinkstock are models, and such images are being used for illustrative purposes only. Certain stock imagery © Thinkstock.

This book is printed on acid-free paper.

Because of the dynamic nature of the Internet, any web addresses or links contained in this book may have changed since publication and may no longer be valid. The views expressed in this work are solely those of the author and do not necessarily reflect the views of the publisher, and the publisher hereby disclaims any responsibility for them.

CHAPTER 1

An introduction

I want to say a big hello to everyone who is going to read this book.

My full name is Min Pin Tootsie and I am a dog. A smooth haired, brown in colour, dachshund. Most people call dogs like me sausage dogs.

My story is about a family of dachshunds, 4 of us altogether. It starts in Nigeria where Bismark was born. He was my dad. After that, it moves to Botswana where the rest of us were born. Then it moves to England, firstly to a place called Fowey in Cornwall, and after that to Bristol.

I have written this story because Bismark told me too, and nobody argued with him. At least though the others helped me.

I am hoping that all dog lovers would like to read this story, and also mums and dads with young children, especially if they already have a dog, or are thinking of getting one, or maybe two …… or even three or four!

Chapter 2

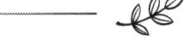

The beginning

It was just a normal Sunday in Lagos, then the capital of Nigeria, hot and sunny, with people enjoying their day off. Maybe going to the beach, or to church, or taking their children out, or off to visit their family and friends.

An ordinary day you might think, but no, it turned out to be a life changing day for Ken and his wife Dezi.

"Let's go to the plant centre" Dezi suggested to Ken.

So it was that they got there mid morning. Almost the first thing they noticed was this dog all curled up on the step leading to the office. They walked up to it. The dog growled.

"Hey mate" said Ken to the dog, "don't worry, we only want to say hello." Ken bent down to stroke him. Again the dog growled.

A voice came from behind Ken. "You have to be careful with him, he's a difficult dog. He doesn't seem to get on with people. In fact, we are thinking of finding another home for him."

Ken was surprised, Dezi too. It was just a small dog, a dachshund they could tell, and it seemed too young to be aggressive. Yet his eyes seemed so distrustful.

The voice had come from the dogs' owner. "It's a shame" he continued, "we had actually got him for the children, but I guess they were too young to have a dog, especially a small dog."

Ken and Dezi looked at each other. They chatted a bit. "Look," said Dezi to the man, "if ever you decide to find him another home, then maybe you could let us know." The man agreed to do that.

Bismark saw them talking. He wondered what was going on. Well, four weeks later he found out. Ken and Dezi had come to collect him. His owner had decided to let him go, and the very same man and woman whom Bismark had growled at on that Sunday were going to be his new owners!

That was how Bismark came to be with Ken and Dezi, and start a life that would take him all over the place. At that time he was not even a year old.

Chapter 3

Plot 31, Temple Rd, Ikoyi, Lagos

Ken lifted Bismark into the car. "That's all right," thought Bismark, "but I wonder where I'm going?"

First stop was the supermarket and then to the pet shop. Bismark saw all the things Ken and Dezi bought. A dog basket, brightly coloured bowls, a lead, a collar, dog food. Even a chewy. "Hey ho," thought Bismark, "this is the life" as he chewed away on the back seat of the car.

They reached Ken and Dezi's house. It was a big double story house with loads of space and had a thatched patio for sitting outside. The front garden was grassy, with loads of trees, including some huge palm trees.

Best of all though was Lizzie the maid and James the cook. "As soon as they came to me, I loved them both" he drooled. "Especially Lizzie. She was just so kind and loving. And she gave me lots of strokes. I didn't even mind her picking me up." Lizzie was from Ghana though she lived in Nigeria. James was from Lagos.

The front garden was a safe place for Bismark to go because it was fenced and there was no way he could get out. At the back though, it was different. Bismark was not allowed there. The servant's quarters were about 25 yards away, where all the maids, cooks and drivers lived, and a pathway that led to the open road. He could easily have got lost, even stolen.

But that didn't bother Bismark. "I still managed to sneak out there from time to time" he admitted, "after all, there were loads of tit bits to be found, and loads of places to have a sniff!" Of course Lizzie never told Bismark off, only Ken did, especially if he had to go and search for him!

A big bonus for Bismark was that though he had his own bed, it was not long before he decided to sleep in Ken and Dezi's bed. Ken was not happy about that, but Dezi and Bismark had their way. It stayed like that for many years until the time when Ken got tick fever.

In the daytime, Bismark got loads of car rides with Dezi. "We went everywhere together," he said, "to the markets, to the shops, to visit her friends, sometimes even on a boat. You always saw us together."

Lots of people got to know Bismark. Dezi put a little red scarf around his neck. "It was proper red," said Bismark, "a bit like what the cowboys wore. It made me look the business. I felt pretty good with that on."

I could tell that those were good days for Bismark.

Chapter 4

Bismark's name

Before I carry on, I want to tell you that when Ken and Dezi first met Bismark, he had another name. It was Popeye!

"I hated that name," complained Bismark. "I really did. Okay so my eyes stood out a bit, but lots of dogs have eyes like that, and they aren't called Popeye!"

Neither did Ken and Dezi like the name. Everybody was agreed that he should have a different name, but what?

Bismark heard them discussing other names. Ken even asked all his friends at the Ikoyi Golf club for some ideas. "It's unbelievable," he said to Dezi, "there are people at the club from Austria, from Switzerland, from Germany, from France, and not one of them has any good idea of a name for a dachshund."

Eventually, it was Ken who came up with the name "Bismark". He came up with that name because Bismark was strong, strong like the famous German battleship from World War 2 days. Dezi too was happy with that name.

Bismark liked his new name. "Definitely much better than Popeye" he said.

It made me realise that choosing a name for a dog is not as easy as all that, especially if your dog is to have any status at all in the world of dogs.

Chapter 5

Walks

Bismark loved his walks. Ken took him every morning about 7, before he went to work, and also every night round about 10 or so.

Bismark stopped at every single tree. There was nothing like exercise. Ken got fed up hanging around for Bismark to do the tiniest squirt. "Come on Bismark, you can do more than that!" he complained to him. But it was no use. A squirt was it. Ken then tugged Bismark to go to the next tree, but that was no use either. Bismark was in charge, it was his time and he would only move when he was ready.

Ken tried to get clever. He would try running down the middle of the road for proper exercise. "I soon got wise to that," said Bismark. "I was out for a walk, not a run! I got stubborn and refused to move. Before long it was back to the trees! Surely, Ken must have known there were no smells in the middle of the road? Surely he must have known what we dogs really want from a walk?"

Bismark did not like going out in the rain. He did not like getting wet. When the rainy season came there were huge storms with thunder and lightning. So the walks were fewer then.

Sometimes in the night walk, Ken would take Bismark to a nearby crossroads where you could buy some suya from a roadside stall. Now only if you have been to Nigeria will you know what suya is. It is spicy meat cooked on a charcoal fire, and very delicious. You get 4 or 5 pieces about an inch square on a small stick and it only cost 1 Naira in Nigerian money, which in those days was about 20p. Lots of people would meet at the stalls, chatting away, waiting a few minutes for their suya to be cooked. You could meet all sorts of people there, but never would you find a man and his dog, except if Ken and Bismark happened to pass by.

"I could smell the suya cooking over the charcoal fire from far away," Bismark told me. "I loved going there. Sometimes I even got a bit, but only a bit. Ken was too greedy about suya!"

Chapter 6

Social graces

Unfortunately, Bismark did not have many of these. It was the way it was for him and it was only when he got older that he improved.

He was very suspicious of all people until he got to know them. All contact was entirely on his terms, especially when he was at home. He thought it was because of his bad start. "I will say though" he admitted, "that when I met people outside the house, like in the street or in the shops, I was pretty well behaved!"

He went through with me all the things that he was especially bad at.

"First, when people were leaving the room and going out the front door, I would jump off the sofa and dash across and nip their ankles. I would lie there waiting for them to go, waiting to pounce! And if they moved quickly, well, that could be another nip. When Ken realised what I was like, he started watching me. I could see him watching me as I waited for the people to leave. He pointed his finger at me and then I knew I had to behave.

Second, I was an absolute shocker if I had a bone. Nobody could get near me, even by accident. Nobody was safe from my bite, not even Ken.

Third, it was a problem if I was suddenly wakened, or if people tried to move me or stroke me while I was lying down. It might have been okay sometimes, but definitely not always, and if it wasn't okay, then I could growl and worse still even bite them. People had to be warned about me. Only Lizzie could do that."

Bismark was a menace when he had to go to the vets. As soon as he crossed the big bridge at evening times in the car, he knew he was going there. Worse still he did not like the vet. Ken had to put a muzzle on him. He definitely did not like that either and he would spend all the time trying to get it off. He growled at all the other dogs in the surgery, and when it was his turn to go in, he growled at the vet. Even with the muzzle on, Ken would have to hold him in a vice like grip if he was having an injection.

"I hated not being in control of what was going on," he confessed to me, "I wanted things my way."

Chapter 7

The beach

Bismark loved going to the beach. "We went Sundays," he said, "maybe twice a month. It was my favourite day out. We got the motorboat from Lagos and sped along the lagoon to a place called Ibechi, about 20 miles away. It was always the 4 of us, myself, Ken, Dezi and their friend Jim. When we got there, the boat was tied up at a little jetty, then we made our way through loads of trees and bushes, and after a few minutes there was the beach, yellow sand stretching each way, as far as the eye could see."

I tried to imagine the scene that Bismark described. The blue sea, the yellow sand, then behind the beach loads of palm trees, and undergrowth, and here and there beach houses nestling between the palm trees. Behind the trees was the lagoon stretching all the way back to Lagos and amongst the trees were little self-made houses where the fishermen and their families lived.

As soon as they got to the beach house, Bismark would start wandering off. Often he would get lost. "It was not as if I felt I was lost," he told me, "it was just Ken who thought I was." Usually Ken would find him in one of the other houses, or one of the fisherman's houses searching for dried up old bones!

Bismark didn't mind going on the sand, but after about 12 o'clock the sand was too hot for his little paws. "That sun almost burnt the sand," he told me.

"As well as that," he continued, "the sea frightened me. All the time there were these huge waves crashing down onto the sand. Boom, boom, they went, boom, boom all the time! It was even too scary for people to go in the sea, let alone a little dog with short legs! Mind you it was different if someone carried me, I was alright then."

For Bismark though, the best bit of the day was when Ken and Jim cooked the barbequeue. He knew that bones and meat were on the way. "No way I was going to go wandering off then," he said, "that smell of barbecue meat was just the best!"

After that, they would relax in the shade, then a bit later go for a wander up the beach and on the way see what the fishermen had caught. After that, it was time to go back to Lagos in the hope that the boat's engines wouldn't break down.

"They did once," Bismark remembered, "because we had to get towed back by another boat."

Chapter 8

Strange business

Bismark was 3 years old when something strange happened. Ken got a tape measure and started to measure him This had never happened to him before. Ken measured how long he was, from his nose to his tail, then how high he was, from his head to his toes, then how wide he was, across his tummy.

Then Ken took him to the vets to be weighed. But would Bismark stand still on the scales? No he wouldn't. "Something was up and I didn't like it," said Bismark, "so I kept jumping off." Finally Ken had to hold him and weigh the two of them together, then take off his weight.

What Bismark did not know was that his measurements were needed to find a dog box of the exact right size for him to be put in a plane and flown to England. Yes, Ken was being transferred to another country, and he and Dezi were leaving Nigeria. As for Bismark, well he would have to stay in quarantine kennels at Gatwick airport until they got to their next country.

And so it happened that one evening a few weeks later, Ken took Bismark to Lagos airport. There was also a lady from Ken's office to help in case of any problem. They all went into the Custom's office and Bismark watched Ken as he did some paperwork. From the worried look on Ken's face, Bismark could tell that he wasn't happy.

Bismark barked. He wasn't happy either. He did not like the look of things, and what was that box doing on the counter? He soon found out. The paperwork was done and next thing Ken was taking Bismark's lead off and lifting him up and putting him into the box.

"What's going on?" thought Bismark. He barked more and more. The next thing he knew was that Ken was saying goodbye to him, then he was alone in this box and Ken had gone. He had never been in a box before. It was a jolly good job he didn't know he was going to be stuck in that box for about 12 hours. "If I had known what was going on, I would never have gone in that box," Bismark grumbled, "never!"

Bismark was alone. Barking didn't make any difference. He waited in that Custom's office for about 2 hours. Then he was put on a trolley and wheeled out to the plane going to England. It was a dark night and inside the plane it was dark. Not only that, nobody else was there. Bismark was alone, no ears for his barking to fall on. He was frightened. His happy Lagos days were well and truly over.

Chapter 9

Kennels

Altogether Bismark was on that plane for 8 hours.

After the plane landed at Gatwick airport, he was met by some people and driven to the nearby quarantine kennels, which would be his home for the next 3 months. Well at least that was what it was supposed to be.

"I hated it there," he moaned to me. "It was absolutely the worst time in my life. My new home was just concrete and wire fencing, with a covered bit at the end for me to sleep in. There were no walks, no friends, just dogs barking, all the time barking."

Before long he became miserable and then sulky, then he stopped eating his food. The people there had no idea how to get friendly with Bismark. Next thing he became thin and had to be given medicine and injections. The days dragged by, then the weeks, then the months. Every day was gloomy for him.

"It was like my life was coming to an end," he told me.

He was saved in time. After 5 months in those kennels, out of the blue the day came when Bismark was collected and put in that same box, and then driven to Gatwick airport. "I was too thin and weak to refuse to go in that box," he said. "Anyway I would have done anything to get out of those kennels!"

He saw the planes, and then the one he was going on. "Oh no, not another one of those," he thought. Bismark curled up in his box. "Where to now?" he wondered.

Chapter 10

Botswana at last

Well, Bismark was going to Botswana, a country next to South Africa. That was where Ken was now working.

This time the flight was much longer than the one from Lagos to London. It was over 12 hours to fly to Gaborone, the capital city of Botswana, a distance of about 5,000 miles. Altogether he was stuck in that box for about 15 hours, maybe longer. It seemed like a lifetime for Bismark. Again he was alone, no friends around, it was horrible for him.

Ken was at Gaborone airport to meet him. He was so shocked to see how much Bismark had changed.

"That can't be my Bismark?" exclaimed Ken to his friend, "is that really my Bismark?" But it was! Bismark was thin, thin like a scrawny rat. There was nothing of him, nothing but skin and bone. He was nothing like the fit and healthy dog that had left Lagos 5 months ago.

Even after all those months, Bismark recognised Ken straightaway. He barked and barked with happiness. Ken got licked and licked.

Bismark ran round and round in circles. It was his first time running since leaving Lagos. He was so happy.

Ken took Bismark to the Gaborone Sun hotel. That was where he and Dezi were staying because there was no house ready for them. It was a Saturday afternoon in December the day that Bismark arrived. It was very hot, because there it was summer, but hey, that was fine for Bismark. In fact it was just fantastic, especially after all those miserable and wet days in England.

Next thing, Bismark saw Dezi sitting in the hotel gardens, sitting in the hot sun, waiting for him. How good to see her. She cried when she saw how thin Bismark had become. But Bismark was happy, he licked and licked her, then he ran all over the place, everywhere. He was eating anything he could find. People all over were giving him food and strokes. He was starving. There were lots of people sitting around on the grass, some people splashing away in the swimming pool, all enjoying their weekend off work. He found lots of people to see and fuss him.

"I was happy again," he told me, "I mean really happy. I wanted to say hello to everyone, everyone I could find."

Chapter 11

The Gaborone Sun Hotel

Bismark's new home was a large first floor flat at the back of the Gaborone Sun Hotel. It overlooked the hotel lawns and gardens. It also overlooked the 2nd tee of the Gaborone Golf club. He was not alone in the hotel. There were 5 other dogs and a cat. Like Bismark, they lived in the hotel rooms with their owners.

"Things were brilliant" Bismark told me. "I soon started putting on weight. I got lots of walks round the gardens. I got lots of strokes as well. Dezi got out my red scarf and before long I was looking good. She took me almost everywhere and I became well known around the hotel. Most of the time I had to have my lead on because there were lots of stray cats around, and also it was quite posh."

In one of the rooms there were 2 dogs living together. They did not like Bismark and one day when they were in the garden they tried to beat him up. But Bismark was tough and he fought them off. It was a warning to Ken and Dezi how quickly trouble could start.

After that, they realised they had to keep their eyes open all the time for possible danger. It was a big hotel with loads of people, also, there were plants and bushes and trees and a big pond, lots of places where Bismark could get lost or in trouble if he wasn't watched.

Ken took Bismark for a walk early every morning. Sometimes, the sun was still getting up. If it was all clear he let Bismark off his lead. "I loved that," Bismark told me, "I could go sniffing all over the place. I soon found my favourite spots and then I would run between them. Ken had to run after me."

Another reason why Bismark liked it at the hotel was the food. One of Ken's favourite meals was T bone steak, and Bismark always got the bone. He would run off somewhere in the room and eat it in private. Hey, that was happiness for him.

Bismark was happy there. Ken also liked it too. He could see the Golf Course nearby and although he did not know it, he was to spend 10 happy years playing golf there. I suppose you could say that the Gaborone Sun Hotel was Bismark's 4th home.

Chapter 12

First house in Botswana

Bismark stayed in the hotel for 6 months. Then he, Ken and Dezi moved to a temporary house because it did not cost as much as the hotel. Something like his 5th home by now.

It was a good sized house with a pool and in a good area in Gaborone. It was winter by then, and it was cold, far too cold to use the pool.

It was at this house that Bismark met one of his absolute favourite people of all time. Her name was Modiane and she was an African lady from Mochudi, a village about 30 miles from Gaborone. She did all the cleaning and tidying of the house, and helped with everything else really. From the moment Bismark met Modiane he loved her, her quiet and kind style was right up his street.

Bismark also met Khoso at the house. His job was to do all the gardening. He got on fine with Bismark, although he wasn't happy when his hard work in the garden was spoilt when Bismark went digging for things!

Modiane had a small house at the back of the garden and also her children sometimes stayed there.

"I was so happy her being there," said Bismark. "I would wander off to her house and look for bits to eat, and if she was off duty I could lie there with her."

As for Khoso, he had his own place somewhere else, but not too far. He had a bike and used to cycle to work.

Bismark was at that house for 2 months and it was a happy time. However, the new house was ready to move in. Well the house was ready but not the garden. It was a mess with all the building works. Other thing was, would Modiane and Khoso be allowed to come as well?

Chapter 13

8, Thamalakane Road

This was Bismark's new address. It was at this house that he was to stay longer than any other place in his life. It was a single story big house with a swimming pool and a huge garden. The garden though was a problem. The mess from the builders was just lying around. There were stones, bricks, rubble, rocks, broken old pipes, broken glass, bits of metal, almost everything you could think of. There was no grass, just weeds. The ground was sandy, not soft like on the beach, but hard.

The good news was that both Modiane and Khoso wanted to come, and their previous boss agreed, so everybody was happy.

The very first thing Ken, Dezi and Khoso had to do was search all over the yard to get rid of all the glass, metal, and sharp things lying around. They knew that if they didn't do that, Bismark's little paws would get cut, especially if he started chasing snakes.

Modiane was really happy. She had a nice house at the end of the garden. It was much bigger than the ones she had before. Later, Ken built a wooden fence in front of her which made it more private.

The other good thing was that there was a huge thorn tree giving her loads of shade. She just loved sitting under it, especially when her friends and children came. It was a favourite spot for Bismark as well.

For most Sundays over the next year, Ken and Dezi went to the garden centre buying flowers, plants, shrubs, and young trees. Bismark also went. He stayed in the car and just barked and barked. "I just wanted to be with them," was his excuse.

Dezi and Khoso spent all their days working on the garden. It was really hard work for them. Bending, stretching, planting all day long. Before long though, the garden took shape and after a year it was colourful and beautiful. They also made little rockeries with desert like plants around, not knowing that snakes would like to live there!

Bismark was a menace in the garden. "I was always digging for things," he told me. "My nose would get really muddy. Often Khoso would tell me off for spoiling his work and making a mess, but his grumbling didn't bother me. I just carried on digging wherever there was something interesting."

The garden needed loads of watering because it was so hot, and also the new plants and grasses had to grow. In the olden days, that would not have been possible because water was very scarce, however, some years back the Government had built a big dam, and even though Gaborone was on the edge of the Kalahari desert, the dam made it possible to have water all year round.

Bismark was always going down to Modiane's house. "Going there and seeing what food I could find amongst her pots and pans was one of my favourite things," he told me. "Other favourite things were chasing frogs and snakes."

Chapter 14

Suzie

By now, I expect you are wondering how it was that Bismark came to be my dad.

Well, about a year after he moved into Thamalakane Rd, Dezi met a lady who had a female dachshund called Suzie. Now this lady wanted Suzie to have some puppies. So she and Dezi had a meeting, and it was agreed that Suzie would come and stay with Bismark, and see how they would get on, and see if they might be interested in making puppies.

When Suzie pitched up and Bismark saw her for the first time, he was shocked, I mean really shocked.

"How on earth could they bring another dog to my house?" he growled. But when he saw that Suzie was a lady dog he changed. Soon he was following her every single place she went. There was nowhere she could go without him. He really liked her and she liked him. He was really happy. From what I could make out, it seemed that Bismark was the best behaved he had ever been!

The thing was though that Suzie only stayed for 2 weeks. The time went so quickly for Bismark. But she had to go. Bismark was so lonely. He kept looking all over the place for her, in the garden, in the house, down at Modiane's. But she was nowhere to be found. "Oh, I did miss her," he told me.

Little did Bismark know that it was all in the plan for him to be a father, but would it work? At that time, nobody knew.

Chapter 15

Tum Tum Maxine

Then something else happened. Just a week or so before Suzie arrived, Dezi was reading the local paper and saw this advertisement:

"Dachshund puppies for sale. Ready in 2 weeks."

In no time at all she was on the phone. "Yes, we still have some for sale" was the reply. Straightaway she was dragging Ken and Bismark to where the puppies lived.

She was so excited. But Ken wasn't. He wanted to wait to find out if Suzie was going to have Bismark's puppies. "If Suzie does have puppies and we get one, then we won't need another dog," he said.

"Two dogs, three dogs, what does it matter?" Dezi said. Ken knew he was in for it.

Now the place was right out in the bush, just sand, trees, bushes and long yellow grass. The roads were just dirt tracks. As soon as they got to the gates, Bismark saw the puppies, tiny little things, playing around in the dust. Some were brown like him, and some were black and tan.

Straightaway Dezi saw the one she wanted. Ken was still not sure, but when he picked the puppy up, he knew he would just have to have her.

As for Bismark, well, he just sat in the car and watched and barked. He was wondering what was going to happen next.

Well he soon found out. About 2 weeks later, the new dog came. Dezi had already decided on her name. It was Tum Tum Maxine, and she was called Tum Tum for short.

Was Bismark happy when she came to stay? "No, I was not" he told me. "She was cheeky and also she was not even scared of me! I used to be in charge of everything, now there was this pipsqueak puppy who did just about whatever she wanted. Mind you, she soon learnt not to get near my food bowl!"

In the beginning, Bismark harassed Tum Tum all the time. His tail would be standing up straight, quivering like an arrow. Often she would yelp when he was too rough with her. Somehow though, it didn't bother Tum Tum, she just happily carried on with life.

Soon though, Bismark could see that even though there was another dog, Ken and Dezi loved him just as much as before. After a week or so he became a bit less bothered about Tum Tum. Even so, he did get a bit cross if she disturbed his sleep, or if she wanted to play too much. After all, he was a lot older, about 4 years older than Tum Tum!

Chapter 16

Good news

A little while later the telephone rang. It was from Suzies' house. There was much excitement.

"Suzie is pregnant and is going to have Bismark's puppies" was the message.

Yes, Bismark was going to be a dad! So it was that a few weeks later I came into the world, and a few weeks after that I went to stay with Bismark.

Now if you think that Bismark was a bit unhappy about Tum Tum coming along, then you can imagine how he must have felt when not much later I came along as well. The problem was that he had only just got used to Tum Tum, and now there would be not just one new dog, but 2 new dogs.

It was a good job that I didn't know how my life would be in my early days with Bismark and Tum Tum, otherwise I might never have gone.

Chapter 17

I arrive

Bismark had loads of worries when I came. For example, would he get the same attention, would he get his same spot in bed, would I nick his food, would there be even more dogs coming?

He would not stop sniffing me. He followed me all over the place. When we played he was rough. Ken tried hard to get Bismark more used to me. He would stroke us both at the same time and show Bismark that there was no need to be jealous. Other times Ken would lie on the grass and encourage us to play. There were a few times when I thought that Bismark was going to bite me, but actually he never did, not then and not ever.

Tum Tum had a different reason for not welcoming me. It was because she was there just before me, and she felt that she was the new kid on the block, and that there was no need for another dog. She was so bossy to me.

"I was here before you and I'm in charge," she warned me. She made sure that I knew my place!

MIN PIN TOOTSIE

Sometimes when playing, she would get jealous if she thought I was having too much fun. Then she would stand over me, her tail sticking up in the air, and make me stop. She was definitely the boss of me. Of course she wasn't the boss of Bismark, he could do whatever he wanted. Nobody bossed Bismark.

Before long though, maybe about a month, we got more used to each other. We did everything together and there was lots of fun, for example chasing each other all over the place, both inside the house and in the garden. Bismark was the fastest, and easily caught Tum Tum and me up, often sending us rolling over and over in the dust.

As for food, he need not have worried at all. We each had our own different coloured bowl, mine was green, Tum Tum's was yellow and Bismark's was red. We each had our own corner in the kitchen, and we were fed in the same order, I was last.

As for sleeping, well, we all slept with Ken and Dezi. Bismark kept his same spot next to Ken, I tucked up next to Dezi, and Tum Tum slept somewhere in the middle. It was 3 dogs in a bed.

That was my introduction. It was tough for me in the beginning, but I did soon learn how to fit in. As for Bismark, well, even he began to learn the value of being in a family, and a new life started for him as well.

Dezi named me Min Pin Tootsie in full, and it became Min Pin for short.

Chapter 18

Modiane

Even though I got a tough reception from Bismark and Tum Tum, there was good news because there was one person who was very happy to see me, and that was Modiane.

"Hello Min Pin," she said, as she greeted me and stroked me. She made a big fuss of me. I was happy.

She was one of my most favourite people ever. Bismark and Tum Tum said the same thing too. She was a very quiet person who never shouted. I know that she really loved the 3 of us. She worked Monday to Friday from 6 in the morning till 2 in the afternoon, then from 5 till 7 in the evening, and then on Saturdays from 6 till 12 noon, Sunday she was off.

She would feed us in the morning and in the evening. We used to hang around her when it was time for food, trying to hurry her up. You know what though, she would not be hurried. Hurrying for her was only when it was time to go to church, otherwise she did everything slowly, surely and peacefully. She talked to us like we were people and we loved being with her. She was the only person other than Ken and Dezi who could pick Bismark up. She had a bond with him.

We loved going down to Modiane's house. We would be on the lookout for bits and pieces of food or bones. The bones were brilliant. We would lie in the hot sand gnawing away. Sometimes Modiane left her dirty pots and plates on the ground by her door waiting to be washed up. If she did, we just licked away. She was not happy if she found us doing that, she would scatter us all away, even Bismark.

Sometimes her children came to stay and we liked that because we were all friendly. Also there would probably be more food around. I did not really know about Bismark's bad habits like biting and stuff till later, but with Modiane's children he was fine, he just accepted them.

Khoso too was friendly with us, but not nearly so much. I guess it was because we kept messing up his work in the garden.

Chapter 19

The garden

I just loved the garden. It was so big. There was grass at the front and round one side, with loads of bushes, plants, flowers and trees. Also at the side was a swimming pool, it was a lovely blue in colour. The back of the garden was just sand, and the other side of the house was a stony path where the cars came in.

Dezi and Khoso made 2 rockeries. They were made on the sandy soil, and various large stones and rocks were piled to give attractive appearance. The only problem was that they became a place for the snakes to go and sleep. Often we would end up there barking away until we got chased off by Khoso or Ken. Mostly they were just sand snakes, and that was okay, but if it was a poisonous snake, like a cobra, they would have to get it out. Khoso had a special stick for that.

The 3 of us went exploring all over the place. We got into digging and looking for things like bones, frogs, lizards and snakes. Our noses piled up with dirt. There would be our 3 bottoms sticking up in the air. Now this was great fun for us, but it wasn't for Khoso. He kind of treated the garden like his own, and definitely he didn't like us digging holes and messing up all his hard work.

"You just stop that" he shouted at us.

When that didn't work, he would try to chase us away. The thing is though that once we got on the trail of something, we did not want to be budged. So Khoso would pick Tum Tum and me up and move us away. But he could not move Bismark. Nobody could move Bismark when he was busy like that.

The other thing is that it was not long before Tum Tum and I realised that Khoso was not as fierce as he seemed and that we could do pretty much what we wanted. In fact he did not scare us at all.

Chapter 20

The gang

So it was that before long we became a gang. We did everything together. We hardly ever saw other dogs. Our house had a big wall around it and so we didn't much see other people either. On Sundays Ken would take us for a walk and we had to find a place where it was safe. For example, big dogs might be wandering around and appear from nowhere, or they could simply jump over their fence and attack us. Neither could we be walked in the bush, you never knew what might be there. A big dog, a snake, maybe a wild pig from the nearby game park, it was just too risky.

So Ken walked us along the roads which had big houses and big walls. Even then, dogs would rush up to their gates barking like mad at us. Hey, those dogs were big, but did we care? Well we didn't. I think it was because we had become a gang that we were brave, even me! We just barked back at those big dogs and tried to charge up to their gates, but Ken would pull us away because we were on leads. There was no way we could be walked without our leads on, it was not like in England, as I will tell you another time.

When people came to our house, maybe friends, or workmen, we just charged up to them, barking away. Often, they would be scared and would start moving away, but that would just make things worse.

"Keep still," Ken would shout at them, "then they won't do anything." Then Ken would come up to us calling our names, so then we knew the people were okay. The thing is, as time went on we actually got worse. Even though we were small dogs, we were not scared of anything or anyone, as long as we were together.

We were allowed to go on the sofa, we could jump up easily, that is except for Tum Tum who needed about 3 or 4 tries before she made it. If Ken was there, I would climb up around his neck, while Bismark and Tum Tum would sleep on his lap, or lie next to him, depending on who was first. Tum Tum needed more jumps because when she was little she hurt her back and had to stay in hospital for 2 weeks.

We only once got separated after that, when we had to live in quarantine kennels in England, but at least that was a few years later.

Chapter 21

The Vets

I liked going to the vets. Bismark didn't. It reminded him of the times when he went to the vets in Nigeria, and getting injections, and how he tried to stop anyone from even touching him. However it was an outing for us and it didn't matter who was sick, we all went.

When we got there, we couldn't stop barking and jumping around. We were so excited that Ken could hardly get our leads on. Ken couldn't put our leads on before leaving the house because we chewed them up, especially me, hey, I just loved the taste of leather.

When we went through the vet's front door, we saw all these other dogs sitting nice and quietly. Well that didn't last long. Our gang mentality took over, there was no peace, we were barking at everyone and they were barking at us. I just couldn't keep still, I nagged and nagged to go and have a nip, and almost all the time Ken was pulling me back. Bismark was almost as bad. At least though he would more respond to Ken's instructions, but me, I was so hyper. I could only keep quiet for a minute tops, then start all over again trying to reach the other dogs. Our leads all the time got jumbled up around the chair legs. It was not a peaceful time for Ken.

Now Tum Tum was different, she would sit under the chair as far away from the action as possible. She just sat still. When it was our turn to see the vets she wouldn't come out. She had to be slowly dragged out on the polished floor.

As soon as we got inside the vets treatment room, we all changed. Would you believe that best behaviour took over? Up on the table we went, one by one, the vet looked at us all, even the well ones. Ken would be talking to us and sometimes holding us while the vet was doing his work, especially if an injection was needed. If Bismark needed an injection, then Ken would put a muzzle on him and hold him very tight, just like he had to in the Nigeria days.

Usually the vet would pass a remark about our weight. "One meal a day is all they need" he advised Ken, "and watch the tit bits!" It was however some years before Ken followed that very important advice.

It was after one of those visits that we remembered him calling Bismark a walking coffee table. I suppose Bismark was a bit fat, but then who was I to say. Besides it was not as if the vet himself looked in good condition, quite short and fat he was, just like us really.

Chapter 22

Holidays

Whenever Ken and Dezi went away, we had to stay in kennels. There was nothing good about it except that the 3 of us could stay in one kennel. I hated it there, it wasn't peaceful like at home. We were supposed to get walks, but if the kennel people were too busy, there were no walks. Dezi knew we weren't happy in kennels, she could tell that we were all hyped up when we came out.

There was a time when Ken found some kennels for us in South Africa. Now it was nice and quiet when we were dropped off, however, when Ken and Dezi came to pick us up a few days later, it was madness, it was crazy busy with dogs and people all over the place. Dezi was angry. "Never again" she told Ken, "no more kennels, we will ask Modiane if she will look after the dogs instead!"

Well, they asked Modiane and she agreed to do that. Ken and Dezi were next going away for about a month. So to make sure everything would be okay, Ken asked the vet if he could pop around once a week to check on us, and he agreed to do that.

It was great with Modiane looking after us. She was always so gentle. And she was always around, whether in our house or at her house. On Sundays though, she was away most of the day because she went to church in her home village in Mochudi, a village about 30 miles away. It was not much fun for us, and we just slept most of the time, but at least it was only once a week.

After a week, the vet came to see us. He came through the open door. "Okay you guys, I've just come to see if you are okay," he announced in a cocky, superior like voice. We didn't like his attitude, not at all. After all, who did he think he was just coming in like that. So we all jumped off our seats and charged at him, barking away like mad, and that was that. He did a quick runner, slammed the door after him, and never ever came back.

Now when Ken and Dezi got back, Modiane said we had been fine. She never told any stories about us. What we did while she looked after us was a private matter. What she did say though was that the vet only came once. Ken was really surprised to hear that because he knew the vet was a reliable fellow. So we all went to see him to find out what happened. "Waste of time going there" he complained to Ken. "They wouldn't let me in. So I left my telephone number with Modiane and told her to call me if ever she was worried. But she never did."

Now this was very strange. Ken knew the vet was well used to treating big animals and going to places far out in the bush. Not only that but he went on hunting expeditions where he would get really close to elephants, lions, buffalo and crocodiles. How then was it that he had no fear of them, yet he could not get anywhere near us? It was a mystery. Despite that, and from then on, Modiane always looked after us, whether it was for a day, a week, or a month. Whoopee!

Chapter 23

Snakes

Mostly the snakes would be found hiding in the rocks or sand, or else sun-bathing by the edge of the house. Just sometimes they would be in the bushes. Finding a snake was good fun, even though they were a bit scary, like when they spat. We didn't know which of the snakes were poisonous. To me they were all the same.

Khoso could guess if we had seen a snake by all the noise we made. He would straightaway rush over with a spade or stick and try to find it. If he saw that it was a poisonous snake, say like a cobra, then he knew that he would have to kill it. There was a lot of bush and open space outside the house and garden, and snakes could easily come in from there.

Some of the snakes I heard Ken call them sand snakes. They were a stripey brown and yellow in colour and the big ones were around 2 to 3 foot long. Now these were not dangerous so Khoso did not bother about them, except to make us move away. They stayed pretty much in the rocks and stones. It was like they had their own permanent home there, and that was where they made tiny baby snakes.

There was a day when we found a very rare snake. We happened to be around the front of the house and there it was sleeping on the verandah, next to where the Security Guard kept his things. As usual we barked at it, then attacked it, and then retreated when it spat at us. When Khoso saw the snake he thought it looked really dangerous so he rushed off to get his spade and came back and killed it.

The snake was greyish brown and its head seemed a bit sideways. Even dead it looked frightening. When Ken came home for lunch and saw it he wanted to know what type of snake it was. He put it in a box and took it to work. "Maybe one of my staff will know what it is," he said to us.

Well they didn't. The ladies ran out of the office screaming when they saw the dead snake, even the men went off in a hurry. Even when Ken told them the snake was dead they wouldn't come back. They wanted that box out of the building. They said it was bad luck. Ken had to take it back to his car and leave it there until it was time to go home. Then Ken had another idea. We all got in his car and went to see the vet. "Maybe he will know," Ken suggested.

The vet was surprised to see such a deadly snake. "Maybe way out in the bush you could find such a snake," he said, "but not in a garden." He wasn't sure what it was.. "I think it is either a Shield Nose snake, or a Grey Shovel Snout snake. It is a good job your dogs found it because they are both very poisonous, and a bite could kill!"

We thought of the Security Guard sitting there all night. Just imagine if he had got bitten! Ken gave us a pat. As time went by, we found less snakes in the garden. I suppose they went to places where dogs wouldn't be bothering them all the time.

Chapter 24

The swimming pool

From the beginning I was afraid of the swimming pool. I did not like to get close to the edge. For some reason, it was different with Bismark and Tum Tum. They were not bothered at all. They would go right up to the edge and even drink the water. Not me!

In the summer we would all sun bathe around the edge, me too, but not as near as them. Our eyes would be blinking away in the bright sun. None of us would go in the pool until one day Bismark lost his balance running round the corner and fell in. It was really lucky that Ken was around to jump in and fish him out.

Ken would get up early before going to work to clean the pool. It was a daily job. There were always things to get out. Things like leaves, twigs, insects, frogs and once a snake. I liked it when Ken came to clean the pool. It became like action time for us. We went charging around all over the place, barking away, digging away, dog's stuff, then when Ken went, it was back to sleeping.

Dezi really loved the pool and used it a lot. Ken not so much, sometimes when he got home from work and then at weekends, when he was not golfing! I liked being out with them. Botswana is at its hottest between October and April, with the sun blazing down from a clear blue sky. At night it was still hot, and you could go in the pool at anytime. Ken and Dezi used to like sitting out at night by the pool, having a drink and their supper. After, they would sit on the sun loungers, and we would jump on with them.

Big storms came usually in January and February and there would be lots of thunder, lightning and rain. These storms could be really fierce. There were even times when we got hailstones, big ones. When the weather was like that we did not bother with the pool, nobody did. The pool got really dirty with all the sand and dirt and leaves and stuff being blown in, and even branches from the overhanging trees.

When Ken went swimming, Bismark and Tum Tum would chase him round the pool. Ken would swim from one end to the other and those two would race as fast as possible to get to the end before him, barking away. Then when Ken got there they licked his face, turned round and chased him up to the other end. After a little while they even ran along opposite sides of the pool so they wouldn't get in each other's way! They just loved doing that.

Now I wanted to join in too. I really did. The problem was they thought it was their game so I was not allowed to. "Don't you get in our way Min Pin," they would shout.

I just watched and did give little chases. Sometimes Ken would move slowly from side to side, then there was less excitement and I was able to get strokes as well.

Then came the day that Bismark fell in the pool. Dezi was paranoid. "That's it," she cried out at us, "you lot are going to learn to swim!"

Chapter 25

Learning to swim and Miss Stiffy

So it was that the very next Sunday we got our first lesson. Ken and Dezi carried us into the water and held us near the pool edge for us to swim to the steps. The idea was that once our little legs got paddling away, they would let us go and guide us along, all the time staying close to us.

Now Tum Tum learnt to do this very easily, she was like a natural. As for Bismark, well, he rolled round quite a lot in the beginning, but after a few goes he started to swim, not much, just a bit.

I was the worst. In fact I was hopeless. I was so scared of the water that I just panicked and sank. My eyes popped out even more. Ken tried everything, he held me under my tummy, he tried to get my legs to paddle, but would they? No they wouldn't. I could not move forward at all, just rolling over all the time. I was so stiff. That was when Ken got a second name for me, it was "Miss Stiffy."

After about 3 weeks the lessons stopped. I think Ken and Dezi realised that I was a lost cause. I could not even begin to improve. One good thing though was that after the lessons, none of us ever fell in the pool again!

From then on, when Ken picked me up, he called me Miss Stiffy. I was not like Tum Tum who was all soft and bendy. I loved people picking me up but it was not easy for them because I was so stiff. As for Tum Tum, well people could easily pick her up, but with Bismark, nobody would even try

Chapter 26

Showing off

With Tum Tum, it was to roll over and lie on her back, with her little legs sticking out at the back and her front legs resting on her chest. Then she would wriggle around on her back like she was scratching it. She would especially do this lying out in the sun. Sometimes she did it when people came hoping that they might give her tummy a rub. She loved that. I found it quite amazing that she was named Tum Tum when all through her life she loved to show off her tummy. It was definitely the most best name for her.

As for Bismark, well he used to like stretching his back legs out behind him and then use his front legs to drag him right across the floor or carpet. He did this loads of times. Also he could go quite quickly. To me he was a bit of an attention seeker, all the time waiting for people to tell him that he was a clever boy.

As for me, I could actually sit up straight. I would sit on my bottom and back legs. All my paws would be sticking out in front of me. I would do this to get attention. "Look at me, look what I can do," my big eyes cried out. I most especially loved it if someone patted my paws while I was sitting up. My whole body just pleaded for that.

Just occasionally, all 3 of us would show off together, it was a bit like a circus!

Chapter 27

Changes

We were at that house for 4 happy years. Sadly though, it changed for us when Ken came home one day and announced to Dezi that the lease on our house had expired, and we had to move to another one.

It was a real shock. Of course none of us wanted to go. I mean how would it be in a different place. Okay, it was only half a mile away, but what about all the changes there would be for us? Dezi was very unhappy and very angry. After all, she had put so much hard work into the house and garden.

Ken got it in the neck. "All the hard work I put into that garden," she shouted at him. But despite Ken's appeals to management, we had to move.

In fact, that hard work had caused Dezi a serious back problem, and she lived in constant pain. It became so bad that she had to go to South Africa to have an operation, and she ended up hospitalised for a week with bone grafts in her neck. After that, she spent most of her days in bed, constantly in pain.

It was really unfair on her to have to move.

Chapter 28

Our next home

Our next house was not as big as before, and the swimming pool was tiny. The front garden was fairly square, there was some grass, and some plants here and there. You could not say that the garden at the back was a garden. It was just hard sand with loads of big trees. Ken used to chip his golf ball around it, and visitors used to park their cars under the shady trees. There was a high wall all round so it was a safe place for us. Ken put up a little fence to stop us getting on the drive and to the gate. We dogs were happy because we had a whole lot of new places to go digging and sniffing!

"It's okay here," we all agreed. But Dezi didn't. She was angry and in pain. She wouldn't even unpack the boxes. They just lay around all over the place. She was so unhappy she would not even let Ken unpack them.

There was good news though. Both Modiane and Khoso came to work with us. We were so happy especially when Modiane walked in. Like before, Modiane's house was at the end of the garden. She liked it because it was bigger. She was not someone to say much, but from the smile that broadened her face we could tell she was very happy.

Despite Dezi's back pains, she tried hard with Khoso to beautify the front garden, but even less than a month she had to give up. So we 3 dogs once again got used to spending a lot of time lying on the bed with her. We were pretty good at that. Even so, at the slightest noise we would leap off, dash to the front of the house, find out what was going on, do our best to attack whoever was there, then when all the excitement was over, slowly making our way back to Dezi's bed.

To be fair, life for us was at the new house was not too much different from before. Lots of barking, digging up Khoso's garden, lying in bed with Dezi, exploring all over, maybe finding a snake, walks with Ken and always searching for tit bits down at Modiane's house. But sadly it didn't last long.

CHAPTER 29

The next bombshell

We were only at that house for 7 weeks when Ken was told he would be leaving Botswana.

It was just too much of a shock for us all, but particularly for Dezi. She was really, really angry. After all, why couldn't we have stayed at our other house for just a bit longer? Sadly there were no answers, and she got angrier.

3 weeks later, Ken made an announcement to us. "Okay you lot, am sorry to say that Dezi and I have to go to England and while we are away, you will have to stay in kennels."

Bismark's face dropped. I could see him remembering about how bad the kennels were for him in England and how he almost died. So Tum Tum and I started worrying too. Ken could see from our long faces that we were all worried.

"Believe me," he said to us, "it will be alright. These are the best kennels I have ever seen and you will be there for only 2 months, not like the 5 months that Bismark had to stay."

We felt a bit better as Ken told us that, and patted us away.

When the day came to go, I found it so hard to say goodbye to Modiane and Khoso. After all, we had been a family for almost 5 years. They gave us loads of strokes and cuddles before we disappeared into the unknown. Modiane was saying "Bye bye Min Pin, bye bye Tum Tum, bye bye Bismark."

That was the last time they worked for Ken and Dezi. We never saw Khoso again, but Modiane we did, much later.

Before Ken left, he did manage to find jobs for them both. They were really, really happy about that because jobs were so hard to find in those days.

So it was that early on a hot Saturday morning, Ken put us in the car and we headed for the kennels.

Chapter 30

We get to the kennels

We left about 8 in the morning. It was already hot. The kennels were far out in the bush, about 15 miles or so, and the last few miles were on dirt roads. They were really bumpy. When the rains came, you could not drive a small car on those roads, it would just get stuck.

After about an hour or so, we went through big gates, then passed by the house where the owner lived, went down a bit of a track, and there were the kennels at the back. A bit further away were some horse stables and just near the office were 2 goats, doing nothing except chewing grass and plants all day long. Even our barking did not stop them.

To me, everything seemed a bit ramshacklety. I suppose that's what happens when you build your own place, miles from anywhere, in the middle of the bush.

We wondered how the kennel owner would be. I mean would he be friendly, would he like us? But we need not have worried. Even though we barked like mad when we got out of the car, he was not the slightest bit bothered. He greeted us nicely and bent down to say hello, and stroke us. Straightaway we liked him. Even Bismark liked him! We could see that he was just a natural with animals.

After some minutes, Ken finished the paperwork and then we were taken to our kennel, the 3 of us all in the same one. It was big, loads of room and had a great big tree growing right in the middle. The tree made it really shady and it was nice and cool just lying there. Ken had booked the best kennel for us! It turned out that for most of the time we were the only dogs there. Except for Christmas time when the place got absolutely rammed.

So that is where Ken left us. We saw him get in his car and disappear off down the track, to fly to England that night. We were well and truly on our own.

Chapter 31

At the kennels

It turned out to be quite a happy time for us. Bismark said it was the best kennels he had ever been in. And when there were no other dogs staying, which was most of the time, the owner would let us out where we could either stay with him in his office, or if we wanted, we could wander around outside. He was quite happy to let us explore all over the place. His name was Rob.

We were safe because there was a wooden fence all the way around. There were loads of bushes and trees and we could go quite far. Sometimes it took ages for Rob to find us. Of course we could hear him calling but it was not like we paid any attention to that. Anyone who knows dachshunds will know that once we get busy doing something, nothing else matters.

As you know I was a bit of a "skiddy." So in the beginning I did not go far away. Of course it was different with Tum Tum and Bismark. They would end up all over the place. Later, I did become a bit braver, but nowhere near like them though.

Sometimes there would be a telephone call from Ken in England. "Hey you lot," Rob would shout to us, "its your dad. He wants to know how you are?" We just barked. Later, Ken told us that he could hear us barking away in the background.

A couple of times, Dezi's friend called Jennie came to check on us. Talk about excitement, we just went mad with happiness to see her. I guess she reported back to Dezi how things were for us.

At night though, we did sleep in our kennel. We had our own baskets and it was warm. True, we did get some rains because December/January was the time for rain, but the hot sun came after and soon dried up the wet ground.

Although I came to like it at the kennels, one slightly big downside was that we didn't get as much food as at home. We all complained about it, but Rob was of the opinion that he seemed to know better. Even when we scoffed our food up in seconds and gave him our "is there any more look?" he ignored us. "Got to get you guys in shape," he said. Another big downside was that there were no places to find any titbits, unlike what we were used to at Modiane's house.

It turned out that we were 3 months in those kennels. Finally Ken and Dezi came back for us. Hey, talk about excitement. We barked and barked. We were hysterical and were jumping up and down like mad things.

Even so, when the time came to go, we felt sad to leave Rob. He too was sad because he had taken us in like a family.

"Come back any time," he called as we left, "you will always be welcome here."

Chapter 32

Another place

Dezi had found us a new place to live in Gaborone. The plan was to stay there for 6 months and then leave Botswana and go to live in France. This was because Ken had become officially retired from the bank.

Like most houses in Botswana at that time, it was a single storey house. Although there were other houses along our road, at the back it was just bush, stretching miles into the distance. The bush had sandy hard ground, with both short and long yellowy grasses, then clumps of bushes and short scrawny trees. There would be worn down tracks where people walked through. Ken never actually walked us there for fear of meeting snakes.

Our new garden was big, with big trees, loads of bushes and plants. It was wild and untidy. There was a disused swimming pool full of stones, concrete, leaves, rainwater, frogs, lizards, sand and occasionally a snake. Ken put in a low fence to keep us away from there. We never found any seriously bad snakes in the garden, just some sand snakes in the rocks.

There was a nice little sitting out area at the front of the house under a huge tree. As well as a table and chairs, there were 2 sun loungers. These soon became home for us. Even if Ken or Dezi were lying on one, we would be there too.

I loved it there. Always Dezi was there and mostly Ken too because he was no longer working. The only problem was that Dezi was not well, she was always home, either lying on her bed, or else sitting under the shady tree. She hardly went anywhere. At least it meant our family was more together there than at any other place.

I found out why we were going to live in France. It was because they allowed dogs to come in from other countries without going into quarantine kennels, provided their rabies vaccinations were up to date. With England it was different, they insisted on putting pets into quarantine kennels for 6 months even if their rabies vaccinations were up to date.

Dezi point blank refused us to go into those kennels in England. "No way our dogs are going into kennels for 6 months," she told Ken.

We were due to stay at the new place for a few months until the house in France was ready. Then we would all go there together. Unfortunately, sad events were to change all that, but first let me tell you about Ryz coming

Chapter 33

The family grows

I will never forget the day. There was this big shriek from Dezi's bedroom. She was looking through a local paper when she saw this advertisement.

"Baby dachshunds for sale. Just 2 left." She was so excited. But Ken wasn't. I could see that from the look on his face.

"No more dogs," he said, "3 is quite enough, no need for 4 dogs! Besides, we'll be going to France soon, so we can wait till we get there."

This made no difference to Dezi. "At least, let's go and have a look," she said to Ken, "surely there's no harm in that?"

The 3 of us looked at Ken's face. We could see he knew what he was in for. Next thing he and Dezi got in the car to go and see how this puppy looked.

They weren't gone long. When they got back, we heard words like cute and sweet, and going to the bank to get money. So it was that the next day they went off again and brought back this tiny new dog. Mainly black she was, with tan markings above her eyes and on her paws.

Bismark, Tum Tum and myself were quite disgusted. After all, weren't the 3 of us enough for the family? I suppose we were quite selfish really. We thought that another dog might mean less attention for us, probably it would yap all day long, and definitely it would be a nuisance.

"Better show her who the bosses are around here," we all agreed. How that worked you will see next.

Chapter 34

Ryz

When Ryz came we all wanted to attack her.

Ken had to hold her and introduce us one by one. I wanted to nip her. We all did. We wanted to stamp our authority. It was our gang culture. We didn't want this little upstart, even if she was cute.

The funny thing was that though the 3 of us were bothered about Ryz, she was not in the slightest bit bothered about us. That made us even more mad. We chased her all over the place. Round and round the garden we went, through the house, out the back door, back into the garden, sending her tumbling whenever we could. Ken watched us very closely to make sure we didn't get too rough.

"Take it easy" he complained to us, "you are too rough. Poor Ryz is getting no peace."

But we didn't. Ken made a decision. "I am going off to get a dog house for Ryz" we heard him say, "she can stay in there."

And so it was that he came back with a nice blue puppy dog house. He put Ryz in. She jumped straight out. "Now look here," he said to her, "the idea is that when you get a bit tired of being chased and bullied, just jump in this house. It's yours, and it's too small for that lot to get in, you will be safe in there."

He tried putting her in again. She jumped out. It was one of Ken's poorer investments. The dog house just became a bit of garden furniture because never ever did Ryz jump in. She just wanted to enjoy all the fun, even if there was a yelp when we got a bit rough, or I managed to give her a little nip.

Ryz was the sort of dog who brightened everyone's day. She settled in real quick, and before long we were a gang of 4. She even had the nerve to climb over Ken and lie round his neck when he was on the lounger. It made us a bit jealous because that was the best spot. Anyway there was nothing we could do because we were too big to get up there.

Very soon, none of us regretted Ryz coming, and Ken never regretted Dezi persuading him to get her. Only problem was that she was a bit yappy, and the slightest sound at night would get her yapping away, and then Ken would have to get up to see what was going on.

Chapter 35

Sadness

I am afraid that stories can't be happy all the time. So I have to tell you what happened in the shortest possible time.

We had been in that house about 4 months and it was right at the end of June. It was winter in Botswana and it was very cold at night, especially that year, with some nights going below freezing. It can be like that in desert countries. As you know, we all slept under the blankets with Ken and Dezi, and when we woke up at night and wanted outside, then Ken would get up, let us out, and stand waiting, shivering away while we did our business.

Ken was going to the Okavango Delta for 6 days. It was in fact a birthday treat from Dezi because she knew he had always wanted to go there, even though she didn't. The Delta is right up in the north west of Botswana and it is a place where they have Game camps and you can see all the wild animals, including elephants, lions, buffalo, hippos, crocodiles and all other beautiful animals, and all sorts of birds.

When it was time to go, Dezi had not been well. Ken was not sure about going but she insisted he must, so he went. Actually he felt a bit happier because she had improved over the last day or two.

But while Ken was away, we could see Dezi getting worse. She hardly moved from the bed and hardly touched the food Ken had left for her. It was cold and the nights were bad for her. She was determined never to see a Doctor again because she had been so many times in the last few years. "No more Doctors," we heard her tell her friend Jennie.

When Ken got back, it was about 8 in the evening. She was shaking so much and it was too cold to go anywhere. She refused to go to hospital. Ken did go and get her favourite meal from the Chinese Restaurant, so that cheered her up. Next morning, Ken called the Doctor, but sadly Dezi died a few minutes before she arrived.

Everybody was very upset, and of course especially us 4 dogs. Ken did not go out much and many friends and relatives came, some even from America, England and Zimbabwe. Uncle Stephen came, we were very happy to see him again, though for Ryz it was the first time to meet him.

It was almost 2 months before Ken felt able to play golf again. Mostly, we all spent our time in the garden, sitting under the shade of the tree.

So that was why all the plans to go and live in France changed. Ken's friends all said he should stay in Botswana and not make any decisions about leaving until later. So that is what Ken did. Bismark, Tum Tum, Ryz and myself were also glad to stay, after all, we were happy there.

Chapter 36

The new gang

After that terrible time, us 4 dogs stayed in that house for about 1 year. We were with Ken most of the time except when he went to play golf, or went out with his friends. We barked a lot when he was away, especially at night. It only took one of us to have a woof, next thing we were all at it. Ken never knew about the noise we made until much later, when we used to hear the chap next door tell him about us.

There was a dog that lived in the flat next to us called Sox. We didn't like him. Ken tried to get us to be a bit friendly, but we wouldn't have it. We just ganged together and kept barking at Sox. Then Ken decided to lift us over the fence, one at a time, to see if on our own we could be a bit more friendly. Well it did work a bit, but then when we were altogether we just could not help charging after him. Fortunately Sox had long legs, so with our short little legs we could never catch him up. I suppose you could say that was the beginning of Ken's efforts to develop our social skills.

We could not go for walks in the bush because of snakes. Not only that, the Game Park was about ½ a mile away over the back and sometimes the wild boars sneaked out. It was too dangerous for us there. Another time Ken took us for a walk along our road, but there was this time when a big dog just jumped over his fence and I got my ear bitten in the fight that followed. So we stayed in our flat and garden.

At nights, there we were, all warm now that the hot season had started, stars scattered all over the sky, the 4 of us each chewing a bone, what could be better? Apart from the insects and frogs, often the only noise you could hear was Ken's radio as he listened to the news and the football reports on BBC World Service, and his happy shouts when Arsenal scored a goal.

Then suddenly Ken stopped us sleeping with him. One time he became very ill with serious fever. He was sweating, shivering, had a violent headache, going hot and cold. The doctor thought he had malaria, but it wasn't. It turned out that he had got tick fever, but it took a long time to discover. Ken just got worse. Finally he remembered he had been bitten about 10 days before, and it turned out there was this hole at the back of knee, which the tick made and had gone in. The tick must have jumped off one of us and onto Ken while he was sleeping.

So from then on, Ken made us sleep in our big basket in the kitchen. We all slept together, with Bismark and me in the back, and Tum Tum and Ryz in the front. Ryz had to sleep in the front because she was all the time getting in and out, even the slightest sound and she was out of the basket, yapping away.

We had become a gang of 4.

Chapter 37

A fire and a surprise

"What's that smell?" we wondered. It was like burning. Ken came out and looked over the back. "Its a bush fire over the back, and its coming our way," he shouted. Sure enough, we could see the sky filling with smoke and flames. What worried Ken was that the fence at the back was only wooden so it would not stop the fire, and because it was hot season the grass and bushes were very dry so everything was burning quickly.

The flames and smoke were getting nearer. I could see Ken getting more worried. He and the neighbours then got out the hosepipes and started to spray water all over the grass at the back. Someone had called the fire brigade and we heard the siren as they came past the house. Maybe now we would be safe, but strangely we could not see the fire engine anywhere. After some minutes Ken went to see where it was. In the meantime burnt bits of grass and stuff were beginning to fly over the fence and into our eyes.

Ken got back. "The fire engine is stuck," he told the neighbours. "It can't get through the path, it is too small. We've all got to get sticks and branches and go over to the bush and beat down the grass before the fire reaches us!"

Well, that was a shock, but off Ken went, not us of course, there was nothing we could do. Soon we heard lots of shouting. Through gaps in the fence we could see the firemen, people and even children coming from everywhere to help. There they were, maybe a 100 or so, breaking off sticks and branches from the trees and bushes and beating flat the tall yellow grasses before the fire could reach them. Ken too.

It definitely helped stop the fire, not only that, luckily for us the wind direction changed a bit, so the fire didn't quite reach our fence. It passed about 20 yards away and then headed to the open land. Ken got back about an hour later, by when the fire was in the distance. Ken was sweating.

"I have got good news," he told us, "first the fire is gone, but better still, tomorrow, you will get a very big surprise."

Tomorrow came. There was a knock on the gate. Ken let the lady in. We were barking as usual, then the barks changed to hysteria as we heard her call our names. It was Modiane, our most favourite person ever. We went mad with happiness, running all over the place, jumping up at her, each of us craving attention from her. It was just about a year since we last saw her, yet we easily recognised her.

Ken had seen her when he went to help with the fire. Turned out she lived about 15 minutes walk away. Now the next good news was that she promised to come and see us every week. And she did. We were always so excited to see her. She always made a big fuss of us. So at least the fire brought us some good luck.

CHAPTER 38

We leave Botswana

Almost a year after Dezi died, Ken decided we would all go to live in England. His idea was to send us there by plane in May, where we would have to stay in quarantine kennels until October, yep, 6 months in kennels. Then he would leave Botswana and take us to his home in Cornwall.

Ken held a meeting. "Now look here you lot, and especially you Bismark, its' just got to be done. I know you won't like the kennels, but I've been here in Africa for over 30 years, and I need to settle down. There is some good news though, when we all get to Cornwall, we will be home, there will be no more changes." Could that possibly be true, we wondered, after all, Bismark had already been in 9 different homes and he was only 11 years old?

Ken had us all measured up. He then gave the measurements to British Airways for the right size dog crates to be made and flown in from England. Then we would be sent to England on the same plane that the crates were coming in on. We could guess it was quite complicated because we could hear Ken grumbling about all the paperwork, licences, arrangements and telephone calls that had to be done. We knew changes were going to happen, but not what they would be like.

Finally, the day came for us to leave. We got in Ken's car, just ordinary like any other day. When we got to the airport, Bismark knew something was up. After all, he had been in the airport at Lagos to fly to England, and he had been in the airport at Gatwick to fly to Botswana. At least our dog crates were really nice. Bismark said they were the best he had ever seen.

Ken put us in our crates. Then we were put on a large trolley and wheeled across the tarmac to the waiting plane. We could see Ken watching us as we went, and listening to us as we barked away. I could see he was upset. Then we saw the plane. None of us girls had seen a plane before. It was huge. What next, we wondered?

Well, I guess you know. Our boxes were carried up some steps and we were put in a special place for animals, though apart from a cat, we were the only ones there. Our crates had little bowls hanging up inside so that we could be given food and water. Ken was gone. We heard a huge noise. Then it was quiet. As you know I was a skiddy dog. I was frightened by it all. Bismark and Tum Tum slept a lot, but not me, as for Ryz, she slept, she woke, she yapped, like that all through the night.

Altogether we were on the plane for about 14 hrs. I was stressed like never before in my life.

CHAPTER 39

England and kennels

There was this huge roar. Then silence. Slowly the plane doors opened. We were in England. It was 7 in the morning, no sun, just gloomy, wet and miserable. We all looked at each other, this was nothing like the hot Botswana we had just left. And worse still, there was nobody around that we knew. Still in our cages, we were carried from the plane and taken to the airport offices where the people from the quarantine kennels were waiting for us.

"What next?" we wondered. Well, we were loaded into their van and off we headed for the quarantine kennels near Newton Abbott in Devon, about a 4hour drive. Yep, still 4 more hours to go in those boxes. Finally we arrived, and then it was more injections, the same old injections that we had done in Botswana! These are the bad things about being a dog.

The rules of the kennels were that the most dogs you could have in a kennel was 3, so because we were 4, we had to be divided 2 by 2. Ken had already decided who would be together. I was going to be with Bismark, and Tum Tum with Ryz. I was happy to be with

Bismark, and not with Miss Bossy (Tum Tum), or with Miss Yappy (Ryz).

Even so, I discovered that Bismark was a terror in the kennels. People could not get near him. He was so aggressive, just barking and pushing himself against the door when anyone tried to get in. I think he remembered the time when he was in kennels and almost died. Fortunately though, there was one person who he would let in. Her name was Clare and she was able to treat Bismark just how she wanted. He loved her. She was one of those people that have that special and gentle way about them. Of course I loved her too. I looked forward to her coming in, it was like the highlight of the day.

The kennels were big enough for us and at the end we could look over the fields. We also had a little covered place where our beds were with a little heater to keep us warm. We could not see into the other kennels because we were too short, but we could hear each other all day long, barking away. Because we loved Clare so much, our stay was quite happy, plus we got walks from time to time.

After a week, Ken flew in from Botswana to see how we had settled in. He visited us several times. Hey, we were so excited when he came through the door, everyone hysterical with happiness. Bark, bark, bark, lick, lick, lick…….never ending. He went backwards and forwards between our 2 kennels seeing us all. But after 10 days he had to go back to Botswana, and we were once again on our own.

Eventually October came and our 6 months in quarantine was over. There was Ken to meet us, his time in Botswana also over. We all said goodbye to Clare, she was even sad to see us go, then Ken put us in his car and it was off to Fowey in Cornwall, all of us to start our new lives.

Chapter 40

Food

There is something about the kennels that I must not forget to tell you. For quite some time, the vet in Botswana had told Ken that we were a bit overweight, well quite a lot actually. Even though Ken thought that we were not all that bad, he had tried by all means to get our weight down, for example no more 2 meals a day, no more milk, tit bits cut back, and a few more walks. Anyway, whatever he tried, it did not seem to change anything.

Therefore, you can imagine Ken's surprise when the very first thing he noticed when he came to pick us up was that we were all slim! He was so happy. Next thing he was asking Clare exactly what it was that we were given to eat.

"Just the "Complete" dog food for small dogs, with a sprinkling of something moist and tasty on top, like minced chicken, or occasionally tinned dog meat" was her reply. "And one meal a day only, and no tit bits!"

From then on, Ken did the same. We never got overweight again. He said that was one good thing from us lot going to the kennels.

So we were loaded into Ken's new car and we set off for Fowey. We were so excited.

Chapter 41

Arrival in Fowey

It was almost dark when we got to Ken's home. Ken had got there about a week earlier to get everything ready for us, and for our new lives in England. Things like beds, cushions, bowls, food, you can probably imagine all the stuff we needed. He had also made the garden secure at the back and round the side so that we could not get round to the front garden. Well at least he thought he had.

"Here we are," Ken announced as we arrived, "your new home." One by one he lifted us out of his car and put us in the back garden. Then something unexpected happened. Ken suddenly got a dose of the runs and had to do a dash to the toilet. That left us on our own to explore our new place.

And in no time we found a way into the front garden, and from there up and down the road. Lucky it was a very quiet area, so there were no cars, and it was winter and dark. There was nothing Ken could do. He was stuck on that loo. He could hear our barks. Then quieter as we got further away. We never thought anything, but he probably got in a right old state. Probably thought we had travelled safely for a distance of nearly 6,000 miles, and then got lost in the last 50 yards!

He had thought because we were short dogs we would not be able to jump off a 2 foot high wall onto the path below. Well we could, and that is what we did, and that is how we got into the front garden, and then onto the road.

At last he was able to come and look for us, frantically calling our names, hoping to see some movement in the shadows, going up and down the road, going up and down the neighbours driveways. Hey, we weren't worried, but he was, we could tell by the sound of his voice. One by one Ken found us and put us into his house. Bismark was the last, naughty boy!

Chapter 42

Settling in

At last we were in our new home. Of course it was sad because there was no Dezi or Modiane, just Ken and us. It was our first time to be in a house with stairs. The others were fine going up and down those stairs, me though, I could get up ok, but I couldn't come down, Ken had to carry me, every time.

The back garden was big and grassed. One of the first things Ken had to do was to have a dog flap made in the back door so we could get in and out. Then he had to teach us how to jump through. Now this seemed to be quite easy for the other 3, but it wasn't for me. Even with Ken helping me, it took me ages to work it out, and it was only after a couple of weeks that I finally got the hang of it. To be fair though, I was a bit bigger than the others.

There was a beach called Readymoney, just a few minutes walk down the road. Ken took us there almost every day. We were allowed on the beach because it was winter. For us girls it was the first time to see a beach and the sea. Not for Bismark though, he had seen it before in Nigeria. We scampered all over the beach, then up to the water's edge getting in but just a bit. Then it was skipping across the rocks. Well that was ok for them, especially that Ryz, she was a natural, but it was not ok for me. I had no balance, and when I did go on those rocks, I fell off. I was so stiff compared to them, so I was left out. Even so, Ken did help me, and I got a bit better, but not like them. In the beginning Ken wouldn't take us on the beach if there was another dog around, he would wait for it to be free.

Sometimes we would go further along to the cliffs and fields where Ken let us off our leads. We loved that. We could charge around anywhere. Often the grass was long, and all Ken could see of us was our heads bobbing up and down, and our tails sticking up in the air. But all the time Ken was looking around for other dogs knowing we could easily get in trouble if a big dog came. Then he had to round us up and put our leads back on.

We became very friendly with Mike the gardener, though in the beginning we barked a lot at him. That didn't bother him though. He came once a week. In fact he had been doing that for 15 years, ever since Ken bought the house. When he was there we would wander round with him and he would talk to us. He became our friend. I have to say that he was a bit more frightening than Khoso, and we actually did what we were told.

Chapter 43

Walks into town

We each had our own leads, and had to have them on wherever we went. As soon as Ken got those leads out, we got into a mad, mad mode. Barking, jostling, each trying to be first, but Ken did us all in order. I was first, probably because I made the most fuss. Tum Tum was last because for some strange reason she always disappeared off into the kitchen to find water or food. Ken never got to the bottom of that behaviour.

We walked into Fowey maybe 3 times a day, but always at least once. It took us about 20 minutes to the shops. Ken found it tough walking the 4 of us, as always we were pulling, tugging, or going in different directions, especially when other dogs came by. Our leads got tangled up time and again. Ken got really fed up trying to untangle the leads, especially as we were all the time moving around.

Ken had to keep us real close to him when cars came by. It was the same when people passed, because at the slightest notion we could dash across and nip. If though he was standing talking to someone, and we were just stood around, generally anyone could come and say hello. It was different with children. We didn't like their sudden movements, or them rushing up to stroke us, so Ken had to really talk to us and gather us in. Not that they couldn't stroke us, it just had to be under our own terms, and Ken's watchfulness.

Why were we so difficult you ask? Well I suppose its because we came from Africa and there we had virtually no social contact with dogs or people. We were just used to wandering round the garden all day long, lying in the sun, sniffing here and there, or chasing after frogs and snakes.

We got to get a bit known around town, and soon most shops didn't mind us going in. We liked it best in the pet shop because the lady didn't seem to mind when we nicked the dog biscuits. We also liked it in the Lugger Inn in the town centre. There was a really big cat who lived there, we all wanted to attack him, but he sat on the bar and we couldn't reach him. Eventually we didn't bother. It was Ken's favourite place. He became friendly with the landlord and even got special deals there!

Chapter 44

Sad news

We had only been at Fowey a few months when Bismark got sick. It was very sudden.

"What's wrong Bismark?" I asked.

"Its my stomach, it keeps hurting me, and my toilet is bad," he replied.

We could all tell he was really sick. Ken took him to the vet and he was given some injections and some medicines but he never got better. A few days later, the 4 of us were sleeping together in our bed in the kitchen, as we always did, when Bismark started crying. It was 4 in the morning. Ken heard him and came down from upstairs and about half an hour later Bismark died in his arms. We all just sat around. It was very sad time for us.

We could see Ken crying. Then the next day he started worrying in case Bismark had got ill from something he found in the garden, and that us girls could get the same thing. So he checked all over the

MIN PIN TOOTSIE

place, everywhere, but there was nothing to give him a clue. Then Ken decided Bismark should have an autopsy. The results came.

"It's okay," Ken explained to us, "the vet has told me that Bismark has died of old age, some of his parts just got old and worn out." I suppose that was fair enough because Bismark was 14 years old by then, which was a good age for a dachshund, it's like being about 91 years for a human being.

When Bismark got back from the autopsy, Ken dug a deep hole in the back garden under a shady tree. Bismark was buried there and Ken put some nice white stones on top with a cross.

Although Bismark was 14, it was a pity him dying so soon after all that time in the kennels, especially when he was so happy in Fowey. He had lived in lots of different places in his life, about 11 places in all I think, plus lived in 3 different countries, and had travelled over 20,000 miles.

I missed Bismark, we all did. He was something of a legend amongst dogs

Chapter 45

Paws/Tootsies

Not long after that sad time, I got a problem with my paws. The pads all started crumbling and bleeding. Ken was really puzzled.

"Oh Min Pin, what's happened to your paws, where have you been to get them like this?" he asked me. But it was just a puzzle.

So it was off to the vets, all 3 of us. I got some medicine and an injection, and stuff to put on my paws, but nothing worked. They got worse. Ken had to carry me all over the place, it was no more walks for me!

It was back to the vets. I didn't like this at all. The vet had another look and said he would read up his books and consult another colleague.

Two days later the vet called for me to go back. He thought the problem was with the way my immune system worked, and that it was not working the right way. It was very unusual. So I got different treatment and the good news was that after a few days it started to work, we all noticed a very gradual improvement. It took a very long time before I got better, and I could only go on short walks and definitely not on the beach. Even on those short walks Ken had to carry me some of the way.

6 weeks later, it was really nice to be able to walk properly again. Nobody knows what caused the problem, but Ken said he did hear of another dog that had it. I was really lucky to have a vet who took the trouble to investigate all my symptoms.

I thought I would tell you this because it was me who had this problem with my tootsies, and my name was Min Pin Tootsie! Now that was quite a coincidence don't you think?

Chapter 46

Kennels again (and the flying dog)

Before my paws were better, Ken had to go to France to sell his house. He was going to be away for 6 weeks, and he managed to find some kennels for us about 15 miles away from Fowey, near Roche.

"First, I'm going there to check them out," he announced to us.

So off he went. "Do you know what?" he said when he got back. "They are really good. You will all be together in one kennel. The people are very friendly and you will get walks every day!" We knew from all our experiences of kennels that Ken could easily tell the good ones.

"And as for you Min Pin, I want you to know that the people there will continue to give you the medicine for your paws." And so it was that everything was agreed for us to go there.

We liked the place and the people straight away, and our new home was quite big enough for us. I loved the attention when they gave me my medicine, it made me feel special, and after about 3 weeks my paws were better. I have to say that although we missed Bismark, it was mega-less stressful without him. All the workers could come and go in our kennel without any bother!

Something funny happened on the way to the kennels. Well it was funny in the end because it could have been such the saddest thing. Ken was going to France on the ferry, and on the way he was to drop us off at the kennels. So his car was full of stuff, mattress, bedding, blankets, pillows, lawnmower, clothes, kitchen things, garden things, radio and so on. All these were needed because his house in France only had furniture, there was nothing else there.

The only space for us to sit was on top of it all. Next thing, as we were turning the corner at Par, I happened to put my paw on the electric window switch, the window opened, and Ryz flew out. Ken did not even know until someone by the road shouted at him. He looked back in his car and there was no Ryz! And then he saw her standing bang in the middle of the road about 50 yards away.

Luckily it was not busy. Ken screeched to a halt, locked Tum Tum and me in and then chased back for Ryz as fast as he could, calling her as he went. But Ryz panicked. She was so confused that she ran the other way! Finally Ken caught her up, and she was okay, just shaking. Can you believe she was not even injured from falling out the moving car. What a fright that was. A lot of people were looking on, probably wondering how a little dog like Ryz could just disappear out of a car window!

Ken picked Ryz up and then waved his hand in thanks to the drivers of the cars who had stopped in the process of chasing Ryz. Thank goodness they did!

CHAPTER 47

Back home

Only a dog could know what life is like in kennels. Same old, same old, day after day. Even so, the people really looked after us. Finally after 6 weeks Ken came to collect us. It was the usual hysterical barking. Ken sat on the floor and let us jump all over him, licking him like mad in the process. He was happy too. He looked at my paws.

"Wow, Min Pin, your paws are better!" I could see the relief in his eyes.

So it was back home to Fowey. It was getting nearer summer now, and getting warmer for us to be outside a lot. Ken was happy that those long winter nights were nearly over. I forgot to mention that in the winter, every night before bedtime, Ken would take us out to the back garden so that we could do our business. Being dark, he couldn't see us, so to stop us cheating, he bought a big torch. He watched our bottoms to make sure we went to the loo. Still I tried to run back and get off that wet grass, but Ken wouldn't have it, he chased me back to the garden.

It was great in the summer, loads of walks for us. We loved it over Alldays fields, just a bit further on from Readymoney cove. Ken would let us off our leads, but if other dogs pitched up, then he would have to collect us. We seemed to think that other dogs were for biting!

Other times we could sit down by the quay and watch all the people and the boats. A couple of times Ken took us on the passenger ferry to Polruan where we could run around by the peak. I was a bit excited on the boat and barked a lot. Nothing like that seemed to bother Ryz and Tum Tum though.

Another thing we had to get used to was having a bath. Often we got all muddy from our walks, also we got more smelly in England than in Africa. Ken would run the water in the bath, then dump all 3 of us in together. Hey, I just wanted out, this was not my idea of life. So I kept trying to jump out, and Ken had to keep pushing me back in. Because of that, I was washed first, taken out first, and dried first. Then I ran all over the house rolling on the carpets. Then it was Ryz out next, and Tum Tum last, she was the best behaved, she just stood quietly in the bath.

In the middle of the summer, Ken had a visitor from Africa. She was an African lady called Kunda, and she was the same lady who visited Ken when he was in France. She was very nice to us all and liked coming for walks and letting us sit on her. I could tell that Ken liked her a lot. She stayed about a month, then went back to Botswana. We all liked having someone else around.

Chapter 48

A political visitor

After Kunda had gone, something we thought rather funny happened.

It was a lovely sunny day. Ken had all the doors and windows open. He was up the top of the house, and us 3 girls were lazing in the sun on the verandah. Next thing, this old gentleman opened our front gate and came in and started walking up to our front door!

Well, we weren't having that. As one, we lept off the verandah and surrounded him, barking away. He was stuck. He couldn't move. He just stood there. We tugged at his trousers, hey we gave him dog madness.

Ken heard all the fuss and came rushing down. "It's okay you lot," he shouted at us, and when he reached the man, we calmed down.

Ken asked the man what he was doing. "Delivering Conservative Party literature," he answered unhappily. So Ken took the man's literature and after a lot of grumbling he left.

Well, that wasn't the end of it. About 2 hours later there was this phone call. We could tell that it was from this man. It appears that one of us had bitten him and drawn blood and he had to go to the doctor's and get a tetanus injection.

"I am very sorry you have been bitten," we heard Ken say, "but please don't worry, the injections for my dogs are all up to date." The man still wasn't happy and continued to complain. "Like I said," Ken continued, "I am very sorry about it but please know there is no danger to you." It was not an easy call for Ken, but eventually the man grudgingly rang off.

To this day, Ken doesn't know which one of us gave that chap a nip. I know though, but I'm not saying anything. One thing though was that Ken had to put a sign on the gate. It said, "Beware of fierce dogs!"

Chapter 49

Back to Botswana?

Around September came another shock.

"Hey you guys," Ken announced, "we're all going back to Botswana. How do you feel about that?"

We looked at each other. "Oh dear, please no more kennels and planes and airports" we asked. But Ken was adamant, he was going to live with Kunda, the lady who came to stay in the summer, and we had to go too. Yep, he must have loved her a lot to go back. It didn't matter to him that we were all happy and settled in Fowey.

The only way we could travel was to fly to Johannesburg, then to change to an Air Botswana plane to fly to Gaborone. Ken had to make all the arrangements for our travel, for our export permits to leave England, for our import permits to enter Botswana, and then permits for entering South Africa as we were in transit on the way. More injections would be needed, and then he had to book all the flights and arrange for us to be collected when we arrived at Gaborone. We saw him spending hours and days on the phone, and doing all the paperwork.

"First," Ken informed us, "you have to fly from London Heathrow to Johannesburg in South Africa. Then you will be taken off that plane and put on a smaller plane to fly to Botswana. There you will be met by Rob, the same man who looked after us when we stayed in the kennels in Gaborone."

This was bad news.

But then, 2 weeks later, something most remarkable happened. Early one morning in Gaborone, one of the Air Botswana pilots got into his plane and deliberately crashed it into the remaining 3 other Air Botswana planes and into the airport buildings. There were fires and wreckage all over the place. He had wiped out the entire Air Botswana fleet of planes. The reason was that he had a serious personal dispute with his employers, and he was very, very angry with them.

The consequence of this was that there were no planes that were authorised to carry livestock between South Africa and Botswana, which meant that we dogs couldn't travel. "Justice has been done," we all agreed.

That changed all our lives. If that pilot had not destroyed those planes, us 3 dogs would have ended up in Botswana, and this story would have been very different. Probably we would never have come back to England.

But Ken was still going. He found us another place to stay while he was away. It was at his sister's house in Sawbridgeworth. Her name to us became Auntie Yvonne.

CHAPTER 50

Three dogs in a car

"You are going to stay at Aunty Yvonne's, and you will be staying there for about 3 months. There, you will get all the love and attention that a dog could wish for." These were Ken's words to us, and we waited to see if he was right.

It was about 300 miles away, and it was our first time to go on a long drive. Ken put the back seats of his car down so that it was flat behind the driver's seat. There was usually plenty of space for us, but not this time. There was Ken's luggage and his golf clubs, and then there was all our stuff. Our dog basket, our big cushion, a big box with all our food, all our food and water bowls, another box containing stuff like our identity papers, our injection certificates, a torch, a trowel to clean up out poos in Auntie's garden, our leads, our towels, tissues and our coats. Then us.

We drove off. Each of us behaved quite differently in the car. Tum Tum looked out the side window for a bit, and would put her head out if it was open. Actually, we all stuck our heads out when the window was open. The wind would force our ears straight back and our eyes watered. We loved it. After that, Tum Tum would go and sleep on the cushion. She was not bothered about the journey at all, and spent almost all the time sleeping.

Ryz loved looking out the window and sticking her head out if it was open. Mostly though, she spent her time trying to squeeze between Ken's seat and his car door with the idea of getting onto his lap while he was driving. Sometimes she made it, and then Ken would have to lift her off his lap and put her in the back. Then there were times when she would get stuck, so Ken would have to either pull her through, or push her back. When she had done all those things, Ryz would go to sleep with Tum Tum. Then when she got bored, she would start all over again. I have to admit though that even with such behaviour, Ryz was not a nuisance in the car.

Which leaves me. I was the one who was the nuisance. I nagged all the way. I would put my front paws on the back of the front seat and stare out the windscreen and nag, like a whimpering sound. I just couldn't relax like the others.

"Ssh Min Pin," Ken complained to me, and I would, but in no time at all I was back nagging away again. Sometimes Ken would get cross and make me join the others on the cushion. That way I kept quiet for a bit, but soon I would be up again. I couldn't help it, even later when other people were in the car, I would nag. I could not help myself. I couldn't go to sleep, always up, nagging.

Whenever we went in the car, it was like that. Ken used to get quite annoyed with me. The only peace for Ken was when we stopped at a motorway café. He would park the car, as far as possible from the other cars, then take us for a walk, then give us a drink and a biscuit. After seeing to us, ken would go and have a cup of tea, and that was pretty much how it was whenever we went to Aunty Yvonne's.

Chapter 51

Aunty Yvonne's

Aunty Yvonne made us so welcome when we arrived, bending down to stroke us, and cuddle us, and calling us by our names. Straightaway we all loved her.

We charged all over the place. In her lounge there were these big glass sliding doors leading out to the back garden. We were just busting to get out there, and when Aunty opened the doors we charged out as one, barking and racing right up to the end. It was like a competition, seeing who could get there first. I never did because I always followed the others.

We really loved that garden, it was huge and grassy, with flowers, bushes and trees all round the edge. Better still, in the mornings there were often fox poohs lying around which we could roll in. When we did, we got really horribly smelly, even stinky, so it wasn't long before Aunty came with us to clean them all up before we got stuck in.

Hey, we were spoilt. There was a lovely sofa, which we could all jump on and off. We could sleep on it and sit next to people if they were on it. There were regular meals, regular walks, tasty bits like the edges of apple pies.

At night, we slept together in our orange coloured dog bed under the kitchen table. It was lovely and warm in that kitchen, much warmer than in Ken's place! Usually Ryz would start yapping early in the morning, long before Auntie's up time. Poor Aunty would then have to put her dressing gown on, come down half asleep, and take us out with trowel and torch and plastic bag, trying to find fox poohs before we did. Then it was back inside and a race upstairs to get into Auntie's bed!

It was actually a better deal than being at Ken's, firstly, he never allowed us in his bed, secondly, we got regular tit bits which were hardly any at his place, and thirdly, he often left us home alone, which was only occasionally with Aunty.

Ken came back after 3 months, we went mad, hysterical with happiness. He noticed we had put on a bit of weight. Aunty just smiled. So it was back to Fowey again. The lady Ken went to stay with came back from Botswana with him and stayed 3 weeks. She loved us too and cuddled us a lot. Two weeks after she had gone, Ken had to go to Botswana again. So for us it was off to Aunty Yvonne's for another month.

Ken was away for a month, then 3 months after he got back, he was off again, this time to get married. Yep, for us it was off to Auntie's again, this time for about 6 weeks. Ken getting married again seemed like a good at the time, but later it was to result in big changes for us all.

But we didn't mind him going, Aunty Yvonne's had become a second home to us, and after all, it was 5 star accommodation!

Chapter 52

End of our Fowey days

Ken got married and came back with his wife at the end of July, and so for all of us it was back to Fowey. Sadly, although we did not know it at the time, it was the last time we ever went back there. A month later the "For Sale" sign went up in Ken's front garden.

We knew that trouble loomed. "Yep you guys," Ken announced to the 3 of us, "we are going to a new place, and it is in Bristol. Kunda and myself are going to start a new business!"

This was bad news for us because we loved that house in Fowey.

First though, while Ken and Kunda were looking for a new house in Bristol, we had to stay in a rented house in a place called Portbury, just on the western edge of Bristol. There was no way around it, we were faced with yet another new home!

Chapter 53

Portbury

We went there in September. It was a nice house, high up on the side of a hill, and you could easily see the waters of the Bristol Channel and the hills of Wales in the distance. There were loads of stone steps from the road to get up to the front of the house. It was quite difficult for Ken taking us up and down those steps. There were times when he came back from shopping that we scampered all over the place, right into other people's front gardens and sometimes through into their back gardens. He couldn't do much to stop us, but fortunately the people were usually out.

At the back of the house, and at the very top of the garden was a wire fence, and beyond that all the woods. That fence looked a bit dodgy, so Ken decided to put a temporary fence across the back garden, about half way up. That way we could not reach the woods.

After a week, Ken's wife had to go back to Botswana to get her daughter, Blessing. Blessing was nearly 3 when Ken first met her, now she was nearly 5. As soon as Blessing arrived we all fell in love with her, we never barked at her or anything. In those days Ken was home most of the time, Blessing was at school, and Ken's wife was at college, and also doing a job. At weekends we were altogether and that was the best time.

Ken liked to take us for walks in the woods. There were loads of trees, and actually it was quite dark when we were near the middle. As you know, I was a bit of a skiddy, and was frightened to go too far from Ken. Not like Tum Tum and Ryz who went all over the place. They could smell the animal smells and then go "chasing the smell". I gradually got a bit braver, and started to join them, but never going as far. The problem for Ken was that if we had a good sniff, we could end up anywhere. He had to keep his eyes open all the time, otherwise who knows where we might have ended up. Once there was a rabbit, but Ken rounded us up in time. The poor thing was so frightened, anyway it was quite safe by then, and we saw it hop off into the bushes.

One day snow came. "What is this?" we all cried out. There it was, all this white stuff, all over the back garden. It reached half way up our bodies. There was nothing like this in Botswana, there it was just sand and sun, and hot. We had to jump up and down in the snow to move forward, we could see Ken and Blessing laughing at us. But we didn't care. It was fun. With the snow all over the place, Ken had to watch us closer than usual to make sure we did our business before we nipped back into the warm house!

Ryz was not so lucky as us. Her hair was long and curly, and the snow got all caught up in it. So Ken had to get it off before she went in. Blessing and Kunda had not seen snow either, so it was exciting for us lot from Botswana. Soon we were all building a snowman, and it lasted about 3 days until it just disappeared.

Quite a difference to the hard sandy soil that we were used to in Botswana.

Chapter 54

Bell Barn Road

Actually, the 3 of us liked that place in Portbury. And it was like a proper family home, with Blessing at school, Kunda working, and Ken home most of the time. So it was a sad time when we saw things getting packed up to move somewhere else. We had only been there for 6 months, and it seemed that no sooner had we got used to a place, then we were up and off again.

Anyway, February 2001 we moved to Bell Barn Road in an area of Bristol called Stoke Bishop. It was an older style house with a lovely garden at the back. There was a fence all round and loads of trees and bushes. No way could we escape from there.

Ken had a new back door made with a dog flap so that we could get in and out on our own. As usual, Tum Tum and Ryz learnt to jump in and out with no problem, but for me it was still a problem. I was so stiff, not bendy like the others. Day after day Ken had to keep lifting me in and out until one day I finally got the hang of it.

"Good girl Min Pin" he said, and patted me on my head. I was happy.

There was a small fish pond in the back garden. We were not too much bothered about the goldfish though I liked to put my paws on the concrete edge and stare at them. Before long, Ken had to put a wire mesh across the top of the pond to stop the herons flying down and stealing the fish. Often you could see those herons with their long necks sitting on top of the nearby trees just waiting for a chance to dive down into someone's pond. It was constant war against the herons.

We hadn't changed in the slightest about strangers coming into the house. For example, there were these 2 men who came to put in a new bathroom. Every time they came downstairs, or came into the house to go upstairs, we would race up to them and bark away. They were there every day for over a week, and every day it was the same, bark, bark, bark. As usual it was always that Ryz who would start it off.

The house was quite busy with people. Ken was always there except when he was playing golf, which was about twice a week. Blessing was always there except when she was at school. As for Kunda, she had started a new hairdressing business and was not so much at home. We also had a young lady living with us from Botswana called Boitumelo. She worked in the salon with Kunda. Often people came to stay, like Ken's son Stephen. We saw a lot of him and every time he came we made a huge fuss, bordering on hysteria. We first met Stephen in Botswana when he came for Dezi's funeral. We always made big fuss of people that we knew, it was like competing for their attention and affection.

This home was a good place for us, and we got lots of walks.

Chapter 55

Walks

About a 5 minute walk from where we lived was the River Trym. It was a pretty place, and the river ran over rocks and little pools, and there were little bridges here and there. The river was only few feet wide, and was in a valley, with hills either side. Ken liked taking us there, it was safe and we couldn't get lost. Mind you a big dog could, he could get lost in seconds. Often other dog owners would be calling and calling for their dogs to come back. They could disappear for ages.

It was here that we became more sociable. It all began when a man who was walking his dog said to Ken that it would be better not to put our leads on and let us be free to meet other dogs.

"They will become better used to other dogs, and learn to play with them" we heard him tell Ken. So it was that Ken took his advice, and bit by bit started letting us off our leads. He had to be careful though because in the beginning we still wanted to charge other dogs, big and small. And though we didn't know it, we could have been beaten up in seconds.

As for me, I still liked the idea of going behind other dogs and giving them a nip on the back of their legs, even Tum Tum did it from time to time. Ken knew he had to keep his eyes on us.

"Min Pin, don't even think about it!" he said as he looked into my eyes. I knew exactly what he meant.

Ken also had to keep his eyes open in case any aggressive dogs pitched up, and if he saw one he would quickly gather us up and put our leads on.

Because of all these things I don't think Ken enjoyed those walks with us all that much. Also, he was worried about our "gang mentality", and having to be on the look out all the time. "No peace with you lot" he used to say.

I am certain that our coming to Bristol was a big step in our social acceptance. We were still miles behind other dogs in terms of good behaviour, but we were slowly getting better. Letting us off our leads more was the right thing to do, even though it was more hassle for Ken.

Chapter 56

76, Reedley Rd

We stayed at the house in Bell Barn Road for 4 years. But after 2 years, sadly, Kunda left Ken and took Blessing to live somewhere else in Bristol. So our house was quiet. Then something else happened. At the same time they left, Ken got a job working at Bristol Temple Meads railway station. His hours were all over the place and from that time on our lives became very lonely.

Now that Ken was on his own he did not need that big house, so eventually he sold it and bought a smaller one about 1 mile away, in Westbury on Trym. As usual, he had to choose one that would be safe for us, and as usual he had to get a new back door with a flap in it. The house he found had a really lovely back garden, and it also had a fence all around, there were trees and big bushes, and a big lawn in the middle. It was perfect for us.

Shortly after moving there, Ken stopped taking us along the river walks. It was a bit far for us to walk there, so he used to take us in his car, until one day some people bashed his window in, there was not even anything in the car to take.

"That's it," he announced, "we will have to find another place to go." So he did. It was around the edge of some nearby playing fields. Lots of trees and bushes there. We soon found out that it was a very popular place for other dog walkers as well, quite a few dogs walking with their owners. By now, Ken hardly ever put our leads on and pretty much put up with us going wherever we wanted to. It was like that eventually, after all the years, we had at last become free. We went almost every day to those fields.

By now, Tum Tum had got a lot slower. Also her eyesight was not so good. She was always lagging behind, and often we would have to go back for her. She was hardly bossy at all now, and with that I started getting really brave. I didn't mind going far away from Ken and Ryz. I became less nervous with other dogs. Tum Tum's decline became my strength.

There was one particular lady that we liked. She had 2 Labrador dogs and she had this sling type thing which she put a tennis ball in, and it went really far when she threw it. So her dogs chased after the ball, and we chased after them, our little legs pumping away. When one of her dogs got the ball, they turned round and came running back, by which time we had got about halfway there. So we turned round and chased them back, barking all the way as usual. Then the lady threw the ball again and off we all went, her dogs after the ball, and we 3 after them. Everybody was happy, the lady because her dogs were getting exercise, her dogs because they liked chasing the ball, us 3 because we liked chasing after her dogs, and Ken too because we were getting a lot of exercise. Also, I think he liked chatting to the lady.

CHAPTER 57

Getting Lost

I can tell you that it's a frightening experience for a dog when he gets lost. There was this time when Ken's brother came to visit us in Bristol and we all went shopping. When we got back, I jumped out of the car as usual, but instead of going into Ken's house with Ryz and Tum Tum, I went into the neighbour's back garden looking for their cat. Ken never noticed I had gone. I went sniffing away all over the place.

The next thing I knew, I was in a new road, with no idea how to get back. I panicked. I charged off down the road, round a corner, oh gosh, I was then on a big road with cars speeding up and down. I ran madly down the road, no idea where to go. I got to a place where all the cars were stopping, so I stopped, and next thing someone picked me up and put me in their car. We drove for a few minutes, and then I was taken to a house where there was another dog. At least I was safe, but where was I?

The people looked after me, and stroked me. Then out of the blue Ken pitched up. I was so happy. Hey, that tail of mine was wagging. I was so lucky. It was such a big coincidence that the people who found me were visiting some friends, who just happened to live over the back from Ken. They didn't know him at the time, but had heard that there was this chap who had recently moved into the neighbourhood, who had small dogs. So they took a chance and went knocking on Ken's door, and that's how he came and got me.

The thing is that Ken never knew I had gone. He was sitting comfortably at home with his brother, and never had the idea I had got lost until the lady over the back came. It taught him a lesson. After that, he always counted us in, 1,2, 3.

The other time I got lost I was at Auntie Yvonne's. Well I never thought I was lost. It was only Ken who thought I had. The 3 of us dogs and Ken went for a walk. In the beginning we had our leads on. Ken took us down the road, off on a path, into the fields and along a riverbank. There were lots of trees and bushes. That was when Ken took our leads off. After that it was downhill for Ken. Before long we all went off in different directions, sniffing along those rabbit trails. Ken couldn't see us. He panicked.

"Min Pin, Tum Tum, Ryz," Ken called and called. Well, I was braver by now, no need to worry about joining them. And so I went further and further away. After some time though, where was I? And where were the others? I ran here and there, but no sign of anyone. Then lucky enough I found the path that we came on, and then the road where Aunty Yvonne lived, and then I saw her house. I just stood at the front door and waited.

Some time later Ken came with Ryz and tum Tum. I saw the look of stress on his face, then it turn to surprise and relief when he saw me. "Good girl Min Pin," he said as he picked me up and gave me a hug. My tail wagged, praise at last!

Chapter 58

Ryz gets lost

I have to tell you this story. As you know, whenever Ken went away we stayed at Auntie Yvonne's house. There was this time when he came back from Botswana to collect us. He stayed the night, then early next morning he let us out, it was damp and dark. He watched us a few minutes while we sniffed and did our business, then he went to make a cup of tea.

Well, I came back in, then Tum Tum did, but after a little while there was no Ryz! "Where is she?" Ken asked us. But we didn't know. So it was out into the garden, with Ken shouting all over for Ryz. But she was nowhere to be seen, and there were no yaps. Ken checked everywhere, next door, then down the road. Auntie Yvonne got up to help. We could tell from Ken's face and voice that he was so worried.

Now at the back of Auntie's garden there was a huge bean field, and a little further a river. These fields were growing thick with beans, and they were up to 6 foot high, you couldn't see anything in there, it was like a forest. Could it be that Ryz had got in there? Ken called and called by the fence. But nothing. Then suddenly…..

just the tiniest of yaps. So tiny you could hardly hear it, but lucky enough Ken did.

Ken climbed over the fence and with his torch went in the field, the ground was muddy and wet. And it got gloomier the further Ken went in. Then suddenly he saw Ryz, all muddy and wet, unable to move and shivering away. She was next to a little stream.

So Ryz was found, she had been lost for nearly 2 hours. Ken eventually found the little hole in the fence, where she must have got through. Most likely it had been made by a fox the night before, as it dug away to get in the garden.

Now the thing is that considering Ryz was one of the yappiest dogs in the world, why didn't she bark when she got lost. After all, she could easily hear Ken calling her name. We all discussed this. You know what, she had no explanation. "I just couldn't do anything, I was so frightened," she told us. Thank goodness she managed to give that one tiny yap. Without that, who knows what could have happened? Maybe lost for ever! She had to have a bath when she got in, cold, wet, muddy and frightened, but happy!

Who could have known that a fox could make a whole in a wire fence, and that the yappiest dog could find no yaps when it mattered!

Chapter 59

Bits and pieces

We loved being at 76, Reedley Road in Bristol. Even with Ken at work for 7, 8, 9, 10, hours a day we were okay. We had the 3 of us for company. We got regular walks to the shops. Ken used to tie us up outside the Coop. People would come and talk to us and stroke us. You know what? We didn't mind. You can see how much we had changed since coming to live in England! Even children could come up to us.

Ken took us everywhere in the car. He flattened some cardboard boxes and laid them in the back, and always one of our cushions was there. He would happily go off to do the shopping or whatever and leave us there, windows half open. Mind you, anybody coming remotely near got seriously barked at, we couldn't help ourselves.

Even with our walks on the playing fields we had become a lot better, nowhere near perfect, but yes, a lot better. Ken could stand and chat to other dog owners while we just stood around their dogs. He still had to keep his eyes on us, especially me, he knew that I was always ready to give a quick nip while no one was looking. Tum Tum though was beyond doing that any more, sadly her eyesight had got worse and she could hardly see. She had also got really slow, always way behind us. As for Ryz, well, she was still a yapper. She had the idea that this would scare every dog she saw, it was a good job they were mostly friendly.

Blessing still came to see us. We liked that. We liked her and always made a fuss of her. Sometimes we would go to a nearby park where she could ride her bike, and we could run after her. We also liked it when Stephen came to stay for a weekend, he always made such a fuss of us. Often he would lie on the floor while we would try to find a gap to lick his face.

There was this time we were driving on the motorway M4 coming back from Auntie Yvonne's. Sadly there was a fatal accident and all the traffic got held up. We sat in the car for about 2 hours not moving, so Ken decided to take us for a walk to do our business and to stretch our legs. It was dark and wet as we walked on the M4 past all the cars. Suddenly, one of the car's windows opened and this chap leaned out.

"Hey" he exclaimed, "its not often you get overtaken on the M4 by a man walking 3 dogs!" It just goes to show that when things are serious, people can still have a sense of humour.

Our car was stuck on that motorway for 7 hours, and we got home about 3 a.m. Good job Ken had food and water for us. Apparently, there was something like 35 miles of cars stuck.

It was easy for us dogs to get out and do a wee, but not for the people, no place for them. And what if it was something else they needed?

Chapter 60

Time up

I expect you know what this chapter is going to be about. It is the end of my story.

It was in March 2005, and I was 14 years old, when suddenly I got this lump on my back leg, it was right at the top and it just grew and grew. Ken took me to the vet.

"It's a tumour," he quietly told Ken, "I am sorry to say that there is nothing which can be done for Min Pin."

Ken was so sad for me, and himself too of course. Very soon though it became impossible for me to go to the loo properly, so Ken had no option but to take me to the vet and have me put me down. I remember him sitting in the car with me on his lap before he went in, the tears falling down his cheeks. I expect he was thinking about my life over all the years.

So it was that in May 2005 that I died. Although I was buried in Ken's back garden, my spirit went to heaven and that is where I have written this story.

When I look back, I remember so many good things, and so many nice people and places. I suppose that going on that plane when we left Botswana was bad, but then don't forget there was the wonderful kennel maid to look after us when we got to kennels in England.

Tum Tum was with me all my life, Bismark for about the first 9 years, and Ryz for the last 6 years, so always I had company in my life. I was lucky like that. When I had gone, Ken was still left with Tum Tum and Ryz, but eventually they came to join me. Tum Tum was buried opposite me, and because Ryz was only 8 when she died, Ken had her cremated, and still has her ashes to this day..

I am very happy in heaven. It is my last home, my 14th home I think. We are all here now, that is everyone except Ken, he is still on earth. It's the beer and golf that keeps him going, and healthy living now that he is back in Fowey.

Printed in Great Britain
by Amazon